★ Fly, Cher Ami, Fly! ★
The Pigeon Who Saved the Lost Battalion

By Robert Burleigh

Illustrated by Robert MacKenzie

Abrams Books for Young Readers

New York

For Madison Keller, with love. —R.B.

For my wife, Alice,

for her love and patience; and to everyone

who risks their safety to help others. —R.M.

Library of Congress Cataloging-in-Publication Data

Burleigh, Robert.
Fly, Cher Ami, fly! / by Robert Burleigh ; illustrated by Robert MacKenzie.
p. cm.
1. Cher Ami (Pigeon)—Juvenile literature. 2. Homing pigeons—War use—United States—
History—20th century—Juvenile literature. 3. World War, 1914–1918—Communications—
Juvenile literature. I. Mackenzie, Robert, 1974–ill. II. Title.

D639.P45B87 2008
940.4'360929—dc22
2007038804

ISBN: 978-0-8109-7097-7

Book design by Chad W. Beckerman

Published in 2008 by Abrams Books for Young Readers , an imprint of Harry N. Abrams, Inc.

Printed and bound in China
10 9 8 7 6 5 4 3 2 1

HNA
harry n. abrams, inc.
a subsidiary of La Martinière Groupe

115 West 18th Street
New York, NY 10011
www.hnabooks.com

It was 1918. Dawn was breaking over the fields of France. But the Great War raged on. The giant guns boomed ever louder as the officer frantically clicked the receiver.

"Come in, Corporal, come in!"

But there was no response. Nothing but static, and a terrible silence.

"The phone's out. We're lost! Our other troops don't know where we are. And we're surrounded!"

"Someone, quick!" the officer shouted. "Take this message—
    send Cher Ami.

He must get through. He must!"

Without pausing, a lone American soldier began

    crawling through the smoky haze.

A straw basket lay on the ground.

The soldier reached inside. "Cher Ami," he whispered.

The one pigeon left! The last hope of the lost battalion!

The soldier held the little creature gently with both hands.

In the dim light, he carefully attached the message to

the bird's leg.

Then he stopped.

He gazed into the wide-staring eyes.

He called out the bird's name.

"Cher Ami. Dear Friend, go safely. Save us!"

Fly, Cher Ami, fly!

The soldier raised his arms and opened his hands.

Cher Ami hesitated.

He rocked back and forth on his thin legs.

He fluttered to a nearby tree,
its branches broken and leafless from hundreds
of exploding bombs.
He shivered. Go. Go.

He took off again, beating his wings furiously.

A German sharpshooter looked out from a nearby hill.

Aha—there! He pointed his rifle.

Bang! Bang, Bang, Bang!

Bullets whizzed past the terrified bird.

Cher Ami zoomed upward with his heart quivering.

Fly, Cher Ami, fly!

Behind Cher Ami, the soldiers of the lost battalion waited,
sharing their last remaining food,
rationing their water.

Again and again, they looked up at the sky.

Will the message get through?

Everything depended upon a small, speeding bird.

Another German soldier, with a trained hawk on his arm,

squinted into the sky!

He unhooded the hawk.

He pointed to the pigeon. Catch it. Catch it.

The hawk's cruel beak clacked.

It soared into the air.

It aimed straight for the distant dot that was Cher Ami.

The hawk's outstretched talons grazed Cher Ami's
   tail feathers.

The pigeon swerved and dove crazily.

He swooped downward, with the hawk in wild pursuit.

Then Cher Ami darted straight toward the bright sun.

The confused hawk blinked. Where was its prey now?

It quit the chase—and Cher Ami flew on.

Fly, Cher Ami, fly!

The small bird raced ahead into the widening blue,

flying a mile a minute,

turning the world below into a green blur.

A loud blast and a flash of fiery light!

For a moment, Cher Ami was almost blinded.

He dipped and zigzagged—but kept on going.

His heart was pounding in his tiny chest.

He fought buffeting winds that tried to beat him back.

He veered this way and that, trying to stay on course.

Cher Ami's wings grew heavier and heavier.

How tired, how tired he was!

Would the flight ever end? When? Where?

Far below was an airplane with painted wings.

Cher Ami passed over a dark river. Is it? Is it?

At last! His keen eye sighted three white roofs.

Fly, Cher Ami, fly!

Circling in great arcs, he swerved and
  descended.
Down and down and down.
With a soft hop he landed on the loft's
  wooden ledge.

A bell clanged, and a soldier
came running.
Quickly, he unfastened the message
tied to Cher Ami's leg:

THIS LITTLE MAP SHOWS
WHERE WE ARE.
NO FOOD, NO WATER.
HURRY! RESCUE US!

The soldier wheeled around and raced off with the news.

The lost battalion had been found!

A loud cheer went up from the American troops.

They would now set out to rescue their friends.

But Cher Ami sat quietly on his perch.

He listened to the cooing of other pigeons in the dimly lit loft.

As he bent forward to drink, his throbbing heartbeat quieted.

His work for this day was finished. Now he could rest.

This brave carrier pigeon had done what no man could do!

He had saved the soldiers!

Sleep, Cher Ami, sleep!

AFTERWORD

For thousands of years, humans have used carrier pigeons to send messages back and forth. The pigeons are trained very slowly. First they are allowed to fly just a few hundred feet from their coops, or lofts, which are small houses where pigeons are kept. Then each day they go farther and farther. At last, fully trained to return home, they are ready to carry messages.

Pigeons can travel more than five hundred miles and still find their home lofts. How do they do it? Some people think they use the sun to guide them. Others think they feel magnetic vibrations from the earth. But no one is quite sure.

In the French language, the name "Cher Ami" means "Dear Friend." Cher Ami was one of six hundred carrier pigeons used by the American Army in World War I (1914–1918). On his most famous flight, the black check cock helped rescue a battalion of the 77th Infantry Division. The American soldiers were fighting inside German lines when they were trapped and surrounded. They later became famous as "the Lost Battalion." It was Cher Ami who carried the message that saved many lives!

Cher Ami carried many important messages. But during this last flight, he was badly wounded. One eye was blinded. And one leg was shot off! Yet he still managed to fly with a message that helped the American troops.

Cher Ami was so beloved that American doctors patched up his wounds. His wounded leg was even replaced with a tiny wooden leg! And for his bravery, Cher Ami received a very special medal from the French government.

Although he died shortly after the war, his story didn't end there. People in the United States and Europe talked about his famous flight. Cher Ami was—and still is—mentioned in many books about carrier pigeons. One well-known poem of the time has him saying: "So with the message tied on tight, I flew up straight with all my might."

And that's not all. Cher Ami is remembered in another way, too. Today, when you visit Washington, D.C., you can see the body of this heroic bird—wooden leg and all—at the National Museum of American History.